Cindy Lou's

Poems from Her Heart

Cindy Malander

ARPress
ILLUMINATING IDEAS
EMPOWERING VOICES

ARPress
45 Dan Road Suite 36
Canton MA 02021

Hotline: 1(800) 220-7660
Fax: 1(855) 752-6001

Ordering Information:
Quantity Sales. Special discounts are available on quantity purchases by corporations, associations, and others. For details, contact the publisher at the address above.

Printed in the United States of America.

ISBN-13   Softcover   979-8-89676-502-8
             eBook   979-8-89676-503-5

Library of Congress Control Number: 2024924726

I dedicate this book to my husband, David, and my family, whose love and support have always been a comfort to me. This is the first book I have ever done. God gave me the words. I just wrote them down.

Contents

What I Dream Of

What I dream of is a world without hate,
A chance to start over with a clean slate,
For the nations of the world to communicate.
That would be a day to celebrate.
To get together with other humans to state
We are willing to work together to make
Our world a better place to cooperate.
To work together in friendship to indicate
We are GOD-FEARING PEOPLE and we cooperate
With peaceful, loving ways to end hate.
This is a big statement you make,
But you have to admit,
It would be great.

A Housewife's Prayer

This is a housewife's prayer
For us wives everywhere.
People think housework
Is a boring snare.
But I do not care.
We have jobs to do
That are beyond compare.
We sew pants and shirts,
Make meals and snacks,
Fold laundry and run errands.
On our hubbies we depend
To run the house
And make our home
A place that's a happy one.
And I consider that a job well done.
That's a housewife's prayer.

The Story of a Fuel-Truck Driver's Wife

A fuel-truck driver's story,
You might think is full of glory.
Keeping farmers' tanks filled
Is important and fulfilling.
If it was not for fuel-truck drivers,
The farmers wouldn't have fuel for their tractors,
Or people wouldn't have propane to warm their houses,
Cook their meals, or dry their coats.
It makes me proud and happy
To think my husband is doing a job that's important,
And that's a wonderful thing to be proud and
supportive of.
That's a fuel-truck driver's wife's story.

Day by Day

I live my life day by day.
It's fun watching cats play,
Thinking to myself what to do today,
Trying not to let my thoughts stray,
Seeing how many bills I have to pay,
What DVD or CD to play,
Trying to run a happy home each day,
Without my nerves starting to fray,
Each morning and evening to pray.
I'm going to have a beautiful day today.
Live day by day come what may.

Happiness Is

Happiness is having a man to LOVE,
That was sent from GOD above,
Who is the man I've dreamed of.
Together we live and LOVE,
To be the kind of people GOD is proud of.
We aren't perfect, that's true,
But we do the best we can do.
Taking it day by day,
We hope to keep it this way.
I hope and pray that someday,
Someone will stop and say,
"They did things God's way."

Human Kindness

Human kindness.
Human kindness is a nice way
To end spiritual blindness,
To help us all show kindness,
And not be mindless
Of others' feelings.
And a new way of seeing things,
And the happiness this brings,
This always makes my heart sing.
This is true human kindness.

My Cat Caesar

My cat Caesar is a real pleaser,
And he isn't a teaser,
And in my eyes he couldn't be sweeter,
And with his LOVE he couldn't be freer.
His eyes are greener than grass in summer.
His fur is black-and-white hair,
And there is no other cat to compare.
He's a timid fellow with strangers.
To them he couldn't be meeker.
If I sound like I'm bragging,
That's because I am.
To have a cat's LOVE like Caesar LOVES me
Is a friendship that a cold-nosed friend like
Caesar does well.
Where will this friendship end?
No one knows but Caesar and me.

Thank You, Mom and Dad

Thank you, Mom and Dad,
For the times we had together,
And in all kinds of weather.
I'll always remember the GOOD times.
They will live in my heart forever.
Memories of my childhood to treasure
That are too valuable to measure.
Words cannot begin to express
My many years of happiness.
I was lucky to have loving parents.
I'll always remember and never forget.
I had the best parents a girl could get.
Although you are in heaven now,
Someday I'll join you there,
And then we can be together again.
You can meet the son-in-law you never knew.
He said he's always wanted to meet you too.

The Love of Family

The love of family means a lot to me.
The reason is plain to see.
Family is the reason we are here to see
Life's ups and downs and troubles and joys,
To play with our children and their toys.
If we didn't have family, we wouldn't be here,
And I think that fact is very clear.
And I hold my family very near.
Let's cheer for family!
And always let them know they are dear.
That's love of family.

The Love of Our Pets

The love our pets give us is timeless.
They are our pets and companions,
And most of the time don't mind us.
We don't think of what our pets LOVE.
That's something people don't think of.
They know our moods and feelings,
And have their own way of doing things.
All they ask of us is a place to live,
And some of our LOVE to give.
Food and a place to sleep,
And they "purr" you to sleep.
My pets are part of my life.
My cat once saved my life.
We need pets to keep joy in life.
That's the love of pets.

The Support of Husbands

The support of husbands is a job
That I took when I married,
Which has never varied.
When our husbands are upset,
We are to calm and support.
At times this may be hard to do,
But with GOD'S help, we pull them through
All life's ups and downs.
But it's not always bad,
After the vows said.
For better or worse, richer
Or poorer, in sickness and in health,
Till death do we part.
That's the support of husbands.

What Love Means to Me

What LOVE means to me is
Like birds nesting happily in the trees.
What love means to me is
Like seeing rainbows in a blue sky.
What love means to me is
Like seeing butterflies in beautiful flowers.
What love means to me is
Like seeing bright stars on a clear night.
What love means to me is
Like seeing a smile on a friend's face.
What love means to me is
Like something you can't replace.
What love means to me is
Like finding hidden treasure.
What love means to me is
Like something you can't measure.
What love means to me is
Like never-ending pleasure.
That's what love means to me.

A Cold, Sleepless Night

It's a cold, sleepless night in my house.
I wish I could say it was quiet as a mouse.
There is a very cold wind blowing.
Tomorrow night it could be snowing.
In February I won't be mowing.
I hope this poem isn't too boring.
My hubby is sleeping peacefully;
I wish I could say the same for me.
Maybe I could drink some hot tea,
Or count sheep—that's cheap.
OH GOD,
I wish I could go back to sleep.

Anger Management

There are ways to manage anger,
To show people you care.
You don't have to be in a snare.
There are ways to compare
That you have love to spare,
And that you forgive is rare.
And you never have to swear.
And that's how you manage anger.

Easter on Auntie's Farm

Easter on Auntie's farm
Always has lots of charm.
And there's no cause for alarm;
The kids were safe from harm,
Looking for eggs in the barn,
Having fun on the farm.
That's Easter on Auntie's farm.

How I Feel

How I feel when I am sad
Is different from when I'm mad,
And I very rarely wear plaid,
Which is really very sad!
How I feel is mostly happy.
I don't mean sappy.
I am happy to think of Pappy.
How I feel is different each day.
And that, my friends, is how I feel.

Making Lasting Friendships

Making lasting friendships is hard;
A person tries and maybe tries too hard.
A person needs a person to be friends with,
Sometimes to share a cry or a laugh with.
We all have days when we need another's view,
And I'm sure they need someone too.
There are days when nothing seems to go right,
Even though you try with all your might.
And just when you say there's no end in sight,
Tomorrow brings new insight.
Having someone to share your day with,
Even though they are a Jones or a Smith,
Sure gives a girl's spirit a lift.

Our Dog Lucy

Our dog Lucy makes life juicy,
And to her we do our duty.
She is a beautiful dog to see,
And proud of her are we.
She is full of energy,
Because she is a puppy.
She thinks I'm her mommy,
Because she is a puppy,
And very dear to me,
And suits us to a tee.
She is our puppy.
That's our Lucy.

Pink Pink Pink

Pink pink is quick as a wink.
It makes you want to take a drink,
Maybe even wear a mink.
I love to wear the color pink.
It always makes you think.
I guess my favorite color is pink.
I wonder if there is a pink mink,
That would make you blink.
That is what you have in pink pink.

When You Need a Friend

When you need a friend,
One who won't pretend,
That would be a GODsend,
And would help your heart mend,
And would be a friend to the end.
It's nice to have a blend.
A person needs lots of friends.
I think this is the end.

Thunderstorms Make Me Nervous

Thunderstorms make me nervous.
I wish they could do us better service.
And it seems the weather service
Can always find a storm for us.
People always stir up such a fuss.
Storms have also made people cuss.
They also are good for rain,
But they are a great pain.
That's why thunderstorms
Make me nervous.

Starting a New Year

Starting a new year
Shouldn't bring a tear,
Or even bring any fear.
It should bring family, friends near.
I hope it will make a smile appear
To all those I hold dear.
I hope this will be a good year.
I'll try to do what is right, my dear.
And have reasons to cheer,
And smile when I look in the mirror.
To do that I'll make extra fat disappear.
To this I say HAPPY NEW YEAR!
That's how I'm starting a new year.

I've Got the Junk-Email Blues

I've got the junk-email blues.
They come in two by two.
The more I delete them,
The more they send to you.
I try to give them a clue,
Tell them I'm through.
Just what is a person to do?
I'm a woman with
The junk-email blues.

I Have Dishwasher Troubles

I have dishwasher troubles, it's true,
And it's really making me blue.
I mean wouldn't it make you blue too?
It always works when it wants to.
Which days are very, very few!
I wish I could show all of you.
If you saw dirty water, you'd be blue too.
I would say more, but I have mopping to do.
Till then I'll see you soon.

When I'm in a Bad Mood

When I'm in a bad mood,
And refuse to be subdued,
With a list of things to include,
To better improve my mood,
The problems come two by two.
Wouldn't it bother you?
I mean what else is new.
These things I feel
When I'm in a bad mood.

A Girl Named Cinderella

A girl named Cinderella
Had a handsome fella,
A story to tella.
This may take a spella.
It always ends wella,
And that's just swella.
It's good for Cinderella
To always end wella.

God Is My Friend

GOD is my friend, and that has no end.
To my needs and prayers He does attend.
My broken heart He does mend.
His Son for us He did send
So that sin would be at its end,
And in GLORY JESUS did ascend
To heaven, our welfare to attend,
To His Father, GOD, my friend.
That's why GOD is my friend.

My Aunt Is a Treasure

My aunt is a treasure
Who's too valuable to measure.
She has plenty of LOVE to spare.
When you need her, she's there.
How can a niece compare?
A lovely aunt so fair.
My LOVE for her is rare.
That's an honor she shares.
Two close sisters who cared,
My aunt and my MOM shared
A sisterly LOVE that is rare.
That's why my aunt is a treasure.

A Friend Is Like a Flower

A friend is like a flower.
They seem to have a certain power.
They hear us hour by hour
And never put us in a tower.
Friendship is a beautiful flower.
To have a friend to shower
Us with understanding power
Means more to us than a pretty flower.
That's why a friend is like a flower.

Car Stuck in the Mud

Car stuck in the mud.
You feel like crud.
My tire has a stud
To get through the mud.
It's not fun, cars in mud.
Then I wouldn't feel like crud.
That's a car in the mud.

About the Author

Cynthia Louise Malander, maiden name Vokoun. Cynthia is a Christian Catholic. She has a husband, David, who is a writer also; one dog, Grizzy; one house cat, Caesar; and some farm cats that want to be house cats. David and Cynthia live on a farm outside the town of Belgrade, Nebraska. Her birthday is January 25. Their wedding date is November 19, 1994.

Her interests are cooking, needlepoint, camping, collecting movies and DVDs, emailing friends, going to my Bible study, and taking care of my husband, David, and our pets. We have no children.

Cynthia has always LOVED poetry. She just started writing poems in the last two to three years. She is putting them in this book so family and friends can enjoy them. Cynthia hopes all who read her poems will enjoy them. When she reads a good poem, it makes me feel warm and fuzzy inside. She hopes you will feel the same way.

God bless all who read my poems. I hope they warm your heart as they have mine.

www.ingramcontent.com/pod-product-compliance
Lightning Source LLC
Chambersburg PA
CBHW050909120626
46554CB00003B/1103